THE AMERICAN FILM DIRECTORS
VOLUME I

BY MAUREEN LAMBRAY

COLLIER BOOKS

A DIVISION OF MACMILLAN PUBLISHING CO., INC., NEW YORK

COLLIER MACMILLAN PUBLISHERS, LONDON

Macmillan Publishing Co., Inc. 866 Third Avenue, New York, N.Y. 10022
Collier Macmillan Canada, Inc.

Library of Congress Cataloging in Publication Data
Lambray, Maureen
The American Film Directors
1. Moving-picture producers directors—United States—Portraits. I. Title.
PN1998.A2L328   1977   791.43′0233′0922 [B]
ISBN 0-02-077220-3   77-8658

First Collier Books Edition 1977

The American Film Directors is also published in a hardcover
edition by Rapoport Press, New York, New York

Manufactured in the United States of America
Printed by Rapoport Printing Corporation
Typography by Cardinal Type Service
Bound by Sendor Bindery Inc.

Comments by Joseph L. Mankiewicz from *More About All About Eve,*
a colloquy by Garey Carey with Joseph L. Mankiewicz, Published
by Bantam Books, Inc. Reprinted by permission of the Publisher.

For Ari
and
My Father

Author's Note

To define the American director was very difficult: Some guidelines for this first volume had to be set. The man or woman had to be known primarily as a director who directed three or more feature films and completed a significant portion of his or her work in the United States or for American studios. To make value judgements on the merit of their films or careers was and is not my intention.

A few directors I contacted were either inaccessible or in the midst of unbreakable shooting schedules, so there are directors missing I would have wished to include. To my great disappointment no woman feature film director that I could contact would agree to be photographed for inclusion in the book.

The filmographies include theatrical feature film directing credits. Short subject, documentary and television credits have been excluded. The directors are not placed within the book by their degree of professional importance. The design and feelings of the photographs guided the order in which they appear.

Acknowledgements

Produced by Ari Kopelman

My gratitude to the following for their advice and assistance:

Marcus Devoe for making final prints for "The American Film Directors," Judy Kass for research assistance on the filmographies, Jane Prettyman and Nina Subin for assistance in preparing the book for printing.

Directors Guild of America, Joe Youngerman, Edward Bianchi, Maurice Cohn, Ruth Ansel, Joy Greene-Markoff, Ring Lardner Jr., Richard Schickel, Bob Bookman, John Springer, Suzanne Salter, Marion Billings, Larry Kardish, Adrienne Mancia, David Newman, Leslie Newman, Joseph L. Mankiewicz, Maria Smith, Virginia Cotts, Louis Principato, Lou DiJoseph, Sam Weinstein, Nora Davies, Creighton Smith, Dalton Trumbo, Lucien Ballard, Robert Surtees, Charles Lange, Jr., Jules Epstein, John Alonzo, Lazlo Kovaks.

All the Film Directors for their encouragement and friendship, and most of all, for my hours at the movies.

Contents

Preface

My Father

I was born in Florida, in the town of Coral Gables, on the wrong side of the camera. The hibiscus bush was my sagebrush and the junglejim my trapeze. There were Indians on the rooftops, romance in the garage, and monsters past the front gate. But even on the most ordinary of days there always seemed to be a movie camera in my father's hands. Sunday was movie going day with my father until I graduated to Saturday with the gang. I didn't know how anything got on the flat square on stage but it didn't really matter; for me the director didn't exist. It was during Battle Cry when I began to suspect that there was a man like my father telling everyone what to do for the camera. But it was not until my own passion fourteen years later for making photographs, in my directorial moments, that I really discovered the director.

While watching an old movie on television in November of 1974 I became curious about its director, Lewis Milestone; was he alive, what did he look like, what was he like personally? I discovered in my research that if there were photos of film directors they were usually indirect and impersonal—hiding behind a camera on set—they told nothing of the man.

Film is the only important creative medium where it is possible for me to feel that I arrived not too far after the beginning. It seemed imperative to me that we should begin documenting our film directors; the men and women who might possibly be a significant part of film history decades from now. There are directors not living who I would have wanted to "see", to be able to have a sense of the man as director and the director as man. With these thoughts I began to search for the directors I could photograph.

I never had the chance to preplan the photograph of any director with the exception of one. They would tell me to meet them at a specific place—and I would never know whether it was their home, office, set or whatever. So I would ride around the neighborhood for as many minutes as possible to find an association in those surroundings for the director, with alternatives for my imagination. There was no set amount of time or rolls of film—sometimes I took as little as 8 frames and other times as much as 3 rolls. As photographers seem to be, the directors were much less comfortable on the other side of the camera.

There was an understanding or sometimes a tolerance by the directors of the kinds of photographs I wanted to achieve. When Hitchcock saw some already completed portraits, he asked where I wished to shoot him. I took a chance and said either on an empty train or a double decker bus. He was in the midst of working on a script and his agent said he wasn't even going out to lunch at that time. But a few days later I received a long distance call from his studio—Universal—asking what kind of train I would like them to put together.

I told George Stevens I would like to shoot him in a vast empty area. Understanding, and without saying anything, he drove his Mercedes straight across a large empty beach, where he got trapped in the sand. We were pushing and bouncing the car, when a group of teenagers came by. They lit into Stevens, saying that old men should not try such monumental things as driving on a beach with a Mercedes and suggested he "go back home to the rocking chair." They were the same group who idolize James Dean and think *Giant* is "far out." George said, "it goes to prove a violin is just a piece of wood unless you know who played it." Stevens had, beside his feeling for film, an interest in photography. He told me that shortly before we die we most nearly resemble our true heritage. George died soon after my photograph of him and in that last portrait he resembles to me an American Indian.

The American directors I found very open—for me no one reputation determined my expectation. There is one thing being a photographer I have discovered. If you must get to the point of who the person is quickly, and capture this on film, call the person by his first name, no matter who he is. It is an informality that causes some sort of breakdown of barriers. I have never found anyone to be offended by subtraction of a title.

At the beginning, when I photograph someone, I talk to them and take very few frames in between their replies. I don't want to make the photograph until I know something more about them, anything. Sometimes I am so busy trying to match up the words of the person to what I see that I don't store all the person's comments unless they are immediately relevant. And yet I must reply to whatever the person is speaking about or I will lose a continuity of personal exposure. I mean, with Arthur Penn it wasn't important to me, in relationship to himself, that he was telling me he had a brother that takes pictures and is always taking his family pictures. Even though I heard all of his talk about his brother named "Irv" I wasn't really concentrating on "Irv." So, I asked what kind of photographs his brother took and Penn replied—"for magazines, sometimes." I asked how long his brother had been making photographs but all the while thinking about Arthur. It wasn't until two days later, while looking at Arthur Penn on my contact sheets, it suddenly occurred to me that the brother who takes pictures and sometimes has them published in the magazines is Irving Penn. But I knew it didn't really matter to my photographs if Jean Renoir told me during our shooting that he had a father who painted pictures.

I have noticed only a few similar traits about film directors—they smoke a lot, they attract accidents to their eyes, they have no set pattern of living, and live long—way past the actors they direct. Allan Dwan suggested I title my book "What? Is He Still Around?"

Maureen Lambray, New York City 1976

The audience is the only final judge,
and I believe in large audiences.

Nicolas Roeg, Director

John Huston
(1906–   )

1941—The Maltese Falcon
1942—In This Our Life
1942—Across the Pacific
1947—The Treasure of the Sierra Madre
1948—Key Largo
1949—We Were Strangers
1950—The Asphalt Jungle
1951—The Red Badge of Courage
1952—The African Queen
1953—Moulin Rouge
1954—Beat the Devil
1956—Moby Dick
1957—Heaven Knows Mr. Allison
1958—The Barbarian and the Geisha
1958—The Roots of Heaven
1960—The Unforgiven
1960—The Misfits
1962—Freud
1963—The List of Adrian Messenger
1964—The Night of the Iguana
1966—The Bible
1966—Casino Royale (co-director)
1967—Reflections in a Golden Eye
1969—Sinful Davey
1969—A Walk with Love and Death
1970—The Kremlin Letter
1972—Fat City
1972—Judge Roy Bean
1973—The Mackintosh Man
1975—The Man Who Would Be King

Each picture with its particular environment and unique personal relationships is a world unto itself—separate and distinct. Picture makers lead dozens of lives—a life for each picture. And, by the same token, they perish a little when each picture is finished and that world comes to an end. In this respect it is a melancholy occupation.

John Huston

Raoul Walsh

(1892–   )

1915—The Regeneration
1915—Carmen
1916—Pillars of Society
1916—The Serpent
1916—Blue Blood and Red
1916—The Honor System
1917—The Conqueror
1917—Betrayed
1917—This is the Life
1917—The Pride of New York
1917—The Silent Lie
1917—The Innocent Sinner
1918—Woman and the Law
1918—The Prussian Cur
1918—On the Jump
1918—I'll Say So
1918—Every Mother's Son
1919—Evangeline
1920—Should a Husband Forgive?
1920—From Now On
1920—The Deep Purple
1920—The Strongest
1921—The Oath
1921—Serenade
1922—Lost and Found
1922—Kindred of the Dust
1924—The Thief of Bagdad
1925—East of Suez
1925—The Spaniard
1926—The Wanderer
1926—The Lucky Lady
1926—The Lady of the Harem
1926—What Price Glory?
1927—The Monkey Talks
1927—The Loves of Carmen
1928—Sadie Thompson
1928—The Red Dance
1928—Me, Gangster
1929—In Old Arizona (co-director)
1929—Hot for Paris
1929—The Cock-Eyed World
1930—The Big Trail
1931—The Man Who Came Back
1931—Women of All Nations
1931—Yellow Ticket
1932—Wild Girl
1932—Me and My Gal
1933—Sailor's Luck
1933—The Bowery
1933—Going Hollywood
1935—Under Pressure
1935—Baby-Face Harrington
1935—Every Night at Eight
1936—Klondike Annie

1936—Big Brown Eyes
1936—Spendthrift
1937—You're in the Army Now
1937—When Thief Meets Thief
1937—Artists and Models
1937—Hitting a New High
1938—College Swing
1939—St. Louis Blues
1939—The Roaring Twenties
1940—Dark Command
1940—They Drive by Night
1941—High Sierra
1941—Strawberry Blond
1941—Manpower
1941—They Died With
        Their Boots On
1942—Desperate Journey
1942—Gentleman Jim
1943—Background to Danger
1943—Northern Pursuit
1944—Uncertain Glory
1945—Objective Burma
1945—Salty O'Rourke
1945—The Horn Blows at Midnight
1946—The Man I Love
1947—Pursued
1947—Cheyenne
1948—Silver River
1948—Fighter Squadron
1948—One Sunday Afternoon
1949—Colorado Territory
1949—White Heat
1951—Along the Great Divide
1951—Captain Horatio Hornblower
1951—Distant Drums
1952—Glory Alley
1952—The World in His Arms
1952—The Lawless Breed
1952—Blackbeard the Pirate
1953—Sea Devils
1953—A Lion Is in the Streets
1953—Gun Fury
1954—Saskatchewan
1955—Battle Cry
1955—The Tall Men
1956—The Revolt of Mamie Stover
1956—The King and Four Queens
1957—Band of Angels
1958—The Naked and the Dead
1959—The Sheriff of Fractured Jaw
1959—A Private's Affair
1960—Esther and the King
1961—Marines, Let's Go
1963—A Distant Trumpet

Robert Altman
(1922–   )

1955—The Delinquents
1957—The James Dean Story
1968—Countdown
1968—That Cold Day in the Park
1970—M.A.S.H.
1971—Brewster McCloud
1971—McCabe and Mrs. Miller
1972—Images
1972—The Long Goodbye
1973—Thieves Like Us
1974—California Split
1975—Nashville
1976—Buffalo Bill and the Indians
In Production—Three Women

William Wyler
(1902–   )

1926—Lazy Lightning

1926—Stolen Ranch

1927—Blazing Days

1927—Hard Fists

1927—Straight Shootin'

1927—The Border Cavalier

1927—Desert Dust

1928—Thunder Riders

1928—Anybody Here Seen Kelly?

1929—Come Across

1929—Evidence

1929—The Shakedown

1929—Love Trap

1930—Hell's Heroes

1930—The Storm

1931—A House Divided

1932—Tom Brown of Culver

1933—Her First Mate

1933—Counsellor at Law

1934—Glamour

1935—The Good Fairy

1935—The Gay Deception

1936—These Three

1936—Dodsworth

1936—Come and Get It (co-director)

1937—Dead End

1938—Jezebel

1939—Wuthering Heights

1940—The Letter

1940—The Westerner

1941—The Little Foxes

1942—Mrs. Miniver

1946—The Best Years of Our Lives

1949—The Heiress

1951—Detective Story

1952—Carrie

1953—Roman Holiday

1955—The Desperate Hours

1956—Friendly Persuasion

1958—The Big Country

1959—Ben Hur

1962—The Children's Hour

1965—The Collector

1966—How to Steal a Million

1968—Funny Girl

1970—The Liberation of L.B. Jones

Martin Scorsese
(1942–   )

1968—Who's That Knocking At My Door?
1972—Box Car Bertha
1973—Mean Streets
1974—Alice Doesn't Live Here Any More
1976—Taxi Driver
In Production—New York, New York

Robert Mulligan
(1925–   )

1957—Fear Strikes Out
1960—The Rat Race
1961—Come September
1961—The Great Imposter
1962—The Spiral Road
1962—To Kill a Mockingbird
1964—Love With the Proper Stranger
1965—Baby, the Rain Must Fall
1965—Inside Daisy Clover
1967—Up the Down Staircase
1968—The Stalking Moon
1969—The Piano Sport
1971—Summer of '42
1971—The Pursuit of Happiness
1972—The Other
1974—The Nickel Ride

I think almost the most important thing about being a
director is to have an immediate answer, whether it's right
or wrong, on something. Scott Fitzgerald said it best in
relation to a producer in the unfinished novel he was writing
based on Thalberg's life. He had the Thalberg character tell
a story about some railroad tycoon who had to make a
decision between which of the two routes to take in laying
the Southern Pacific Railroad. There were obviously so
many factors that nobody knew what would happen if you
put the railroad through this part of the wilderness or that
part of the wilderness. Nobody could make that decision, but
there was a man who just said, "that way", and that made
him a tycoon. That's what a director has to do.

Ring Lardner Jr., Screenwriter

Stanley Donen
(1924–   )

For me, directing films is like having sex;
when it's good, it's very good;
but when it's bad, it's still good!

Stanley Donen

Howard Hawks
(1896–   )

1926—The Road to Glory
1926—Fig Leaves
1927—The Cradle Snatchers
1927—Paid to Love
1928—A Girl in Every Port
1928—Fazil
1928—The Air Circus
1929—Trent's Last Case
1930—The Dawn Patrol
1931—The Criminal Code
1932—The Crowd Roars
1932—Scarface
1932—Tiger Shark
1933—Today We Live
1934—Twentieth Century
1934—Viva Villa (co-director)
1935—Barbary Coast
1936—Ceiling Zero
1936—The Road to Glory
1936—Come and Get It (co-director)
1938—Bringing Up Baby
1939—Only Angels Have Wings
1940—His Girl Friday
1941—Sergeant York
1941—Ball of Fire
1942—Air Force
1944—To Have and Have Not
1946—The Big Sleep
1948—A Song Is Born
1948—Red River
1949—I Was a Male War Bride
1952—The Big Sky
1952—Monkey Business
1952—O. Henry's Full House (1 episode)
1953—Gentlemen Prefer Blondes
1955—Land of the Pharaohs
1958—Rio Bravo
1962—Hatari!
1964—Man's Favorite Sport
1965—Red Line 7000
1966—El Dorado
1970—Rio Lobo

Rouben Mamoulian
(1897–   )

1929—Applause
1931—City Streets
1932—Dr. Jekyll and Mr. Hyde
1932—Love Me Tonight
1933—Song of Songs
1933—Queen Christina
1934—We Live Again
1935—Becky Sharp
1936—The Gay Desperado
1937—High, Wide and Handsome
1939—Golden Boy
1940—The Mark of Zorro
1941—Blood and Sand
1942—Rings on Her Fingers
1948—Summer Holiday
1957—Silk Stockings

Sydney Pollack
(1934–   )

1965—The Slender Thread
1966—This Property is Condemned
1968—The Scalphunters
1969—Castle Keep
1969—They Shoot Horses, Don't They?
1972—Jeremiah Johnson
1973—The Way We Were
1974—The Yakuza
1975—Three Days of the Condor
In Production—Bobby Deerfield

Martin Ritt
(1919–   )

1956—Edge of the City
1957—No Down Payment
1957—The Long Hot Summer
1959—The Sound and the Fury
1959—The Black Orchid
1960—Five Branded Women
1961—Paris Blues
1962—Adventures of a Young Man
1963—Hud
1964—The Outrage
1965—The Spy Who Came in from the Cold
1967—Hombre
1968—The Brotherhood
1969—The Molly Maguires
1970—The Great White Hope
1972—Sounder
1972—Pete 'n Tillie
1974—Conrack
1976—The Front
In Production—Casey's Shadow

Don Siegel
(1912–   )

1946—The Verdict
1948—Night Unto Night
1949—The Big Steal
1952—Duel at Silver Creek
1952—No Time for Flowers
1953—Count the Hours
1954—China Venture
1954—Riot in Cell Block Eleven
1955—Prive Hell 36
1955—An Annapolis Story
1956—Invasion of the Body Snatchers
1957—Crime in the Streets
1957—Spanish Affair
1957—Baby Face Nelson
1958—The Line Up
1958—The Gun Runners
1959—The Hound Dog Man
1959—Edge of Eternity
1960—Flaming Star
1962—Hell is for Heroes
1964—The Killers
1968—Madigan
1968—Coogan's Bluff
1969—Death of a Gunfighter (co-director)
1970—Two Mules for Sister Sara
1971—The Beguiled
1972—Dirty Harry
1973—Charlie Varrick
1974—The Black Windmill
1976—The Shootist

Jerry Schatzberg
(1927–   )

1971—Puzzle of a Downfall Child
1971—The Panic in Needle Park
1973—Scarecrow
1976—Dandy, the All American Girl

Frank Perry
(1930–   )

1963—David and Lisa
1965—Ladybug, Ladybug
1968—The Swimmer
1968—Trilogy
1969—Last Summer
1970—Diary of a Mad Housewife
1971—Doc
1972—Play It as It Lays
1974—Man on a Swing
1975—Rancho De Luxe

Jean Renoir
(1894–   )

1924—La Fille de l'Eau
1926—Nana
1927—Charleston
1927—Marquitta
1928—La Petite Marchande d'Allumettes
1928—Tire-au-Flanc
1929—Le Tournoi dans la Cité
1929—Le Bled
1931—On Purge Bébé
1931—La Chienne
1932—La Nuit du Carrefour
1932—Boudu Sauvé des Eaux
1933—Chotard et Cie
1934—Toni
1934—Madame Bovary
1935—Le Crime de Monsieur Lange
1936—La Vie est à Nous
1936—Les Bas Fonds
1936—Une Partie de Campagne
1937—La Grande Illusion
1938—La Marseillaise
1938—La Bête Humaine
1939—La Règle du Jeu
1941—Swamp Water
1943—This Land Is Mine
1944—The Southerner
1945—The Diary of a Chambermaid
1947—The Woman on the Beach
1951—The River
1953—The Golden Coach
1955—French Can Can
1956—Elena et les Hommes
1959—Le Déjeuner sur l'Herbe
1961—Le Testament du Dr. Cordelier
1961—Le Caporal Epinglé

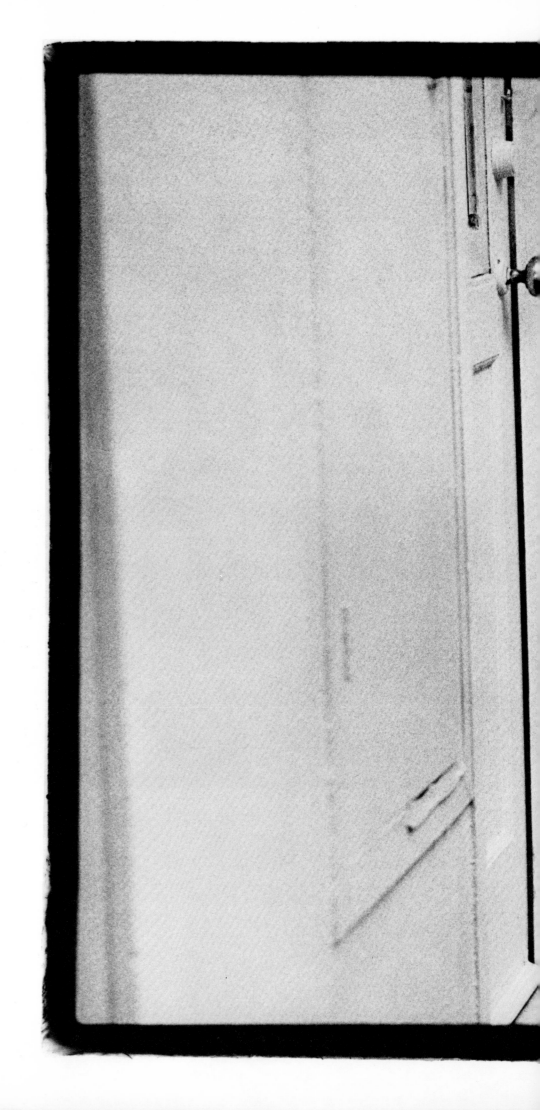

Gordon Parks
(1912–   )

1968—The Learning Tree
1971—Shaft
1972—Shaft's Big Score
1976—Leadbelly

Clarence Brown

(1890–   )

1920—The Great Redeemer
1922—The Light in the Dark
1923—Don't Marry for Money
1923—The Acquittal
1924—The Signal Tower
1924—Butterfly
1925—Smouldering Fires
1925—The Eagle
1925—The Goose Woman
1926—Kiki
1926—Flesh and the Devil
1928—The Trail Of '98
1929—Wonder of Women
1929—A Woman of Affairs
1929—Navy Blues
1930—Anna Christie
1930—Romance
1931—Inspiration
1931—A Free Soul
1931—Possessed
1932—Emma
1932—Letty Lynton
1932—The Son-Daughter
1933—Looking Forward
1933—Night Flight

1934—Sadie McKee
1934—Chained
1935—Anna Karenina
1935—Ah Wilderness!
1936—Wife versus Secretary
1936—The Gorgeous Hussy
1937—Conquest
1938—Of Human Hearts
1938—Idiot's Delight
1939—The Rains Came
1940—Edison the Man
1941—Come Live with Me
1941—They Met in Bombay
1943—The Human Comedy
1944—The White Cliffs of Dover
1944—National Velvet
1946—The Yearling
1947—Song of Love
1949—Intruder in the Dust
1950—To Please a Lady
1951—It's a Big Country
        (1 episode)
1951—Angels in the Outfield
1951—When in Rome
1952—Plymouth Adventure

Henry King
(1896–   )

1916—Who Pays?	1931—Merely Mary Ann
1917—Southern Pride	1931—Over the Hill
1917—A Game of Wits	1932—The Woman in Room 13
1917—The Mate of the Sally Ann	1933—State Fair
1918—Beauty and the Rogue	1933—I Loved You Wednesday
1918—Powers that Pray	1934—Carolina
1918—Hearts or Diamonds	1934—Marie Galante
1918—The Locked Heart	1935—Way Down East
1918—When a Man Rides Alone	1935—One More Spring
1918—Hobbs in a Hurry	1936—Lloyd's of London
1918—All the World to Nothing	1936—Ramona
1919—Brass Buttons	1936—The Country Doctor
1919—Some Liar	1937—Seventh Heaven
1919—Where the West Begins	1937—In Old Chicago
1919—This Hero Stuff	1938—Alexander's Ragtime Band
1919—Six Feet Four	1939—Jesse James
1919—A Fugitive from Matrimony	1939—Stanley and Livingstone
1919—Haunting Shadows	1940—Little Old New York
1919—23½ Hours Leave	1940—Chad Hanna
1919—A Sporting Chance	1940—Maryland
1920—One Hour Before Dawn	1941—A Yank in the R.A.F.
1920—Dice of Destiny	1941—Remember the Day
1920—Help Wanted, Male	1942—The Black Swan
1920—When We Were 21	1943—The Song of Bernadette
1921—Mistress of Shenstone	1944—Wilson
1921—Salvage	1945—A Bell for Adano
1921—The Sting of the Lash	1946—Margie
1921—Tol'able David	1947—Captain from Castile
1922—The Seventh Day	1948—Deep Waters
1922—The Bond Boy	1949—Prince of Foxes
1922—Sonny	1949—Twelve O'Clock High
1923—Fury	1950—The Gunfighter
1923—The White Sister	1951—I'd Climb the Highest Mountain
1924—Romola	1951—David and Bathsheba
1925—Stella Dallas	1952—Wait till the Sun Shines, Nellie
1925—Sackcloth and Scarlet	1952—The Snows of Kilimanjaro
1925—Any Woman	1952—O. Henry's Full House
1926—Partners Again	(1 episode)
1926—The Winning of	1953—King of the Khyber Rifles
Barbara Worth	1955—Untamed
1927—The Magic Flame	1955—Love is a Many Splendored Thing
1928—The Woman Disputed	1956—Carousel
(co-director)	1957—The Sun Also Rises
1929—She Goes to War	1958—The Bravados
1929—Hell Harbor	1959—This Earth is Mine
1930—Eyes of the World	1959—Beloved Infidel
1930—Lightnin'	1961—Tender is the Night

Sidney Lumet
(1924–   )

1957—Twelve Angry Men
1958—Stage Struck
1959—That Kind of Woman
1960—The Fugitive Kind
1961—A View From the Bridge
1962—Long Day's Journey into Night
1964—Fail Safe
1965—The Pawnbroker
1965—The Hill
1965—The Group
1966—The Deadly Affair
1968—Bye Bye Braverman
1968—The Sea Gull
1969—The Appointment
1970—The Last of the Mobile Hot Shots
1972—The Anderson Tapes
1972—The Offence
1972—Child's Play
1973—Serpico
1974—Lovin' Molly
1974—Murder on the Orient Express
1975—Dog Day Afternoon
1976—Network
In Production—They Shall Not Pass

There may be six or seven great pictures, maybe 10 since
the beginning of films and the rest is entertainment,
perfectly worthwhile entertainment that can do some good
sometimes and some evil sometimes. But we'll never be
saved by pictures nor do I think we will ever be destroyed
by them.

Dalton Trumbo, Screenwriter

Elia Kazan
(1909–   )

1945—A Tree Grows in Brooklyn
1947—The Sea of Grass
1947—Boomerang
1947—Gentleman's Agreement
1949—Pinky
1950—Panic in the Streets
1951—A Streetcar Named Desire
1952—Viva Zapata!
1953—Man on a Tightrope
1954—On the Waterfront
1955—East of Eden
1956—Baby Doll
1957—A Face in the Crowd
1960—Wild River
1961—Splendor in the Grass
1963—America America
1969—The Arrangement
1972—The Visitors
1976—The Last Tycoon

Joshua Logan
(1908–   )

1938—I Met My Love Again
           (co-director)
1955—Picnic
1956—Bus Stop
1957—Sayonara
1958—South Pacific
1960—Tall Story
1961—Fanny
1964—Ensign Pulver
1967—Camelot
1969—Paint Your Wagon

Bob Fosse
(1927–   )

1968—Sweet Charity
1972—Cabaret
1974—Lenny

The best directors are artists with a touch of show biz hack in them. Me? I'm a show biz hack with a touch of artist in me.

Bob Fosse

George Marshall
(1891–1975)

1916—Love's Lariat
1920—The Adventures of Ruth
1920—Prairie Trails
1921—The Haunted Valley
1932—Pack up Your Troubles (co-director)
1934—Ever Since Eve
1934—Wild Gold
1934—She Learned about Sailors
1934—365 Days in Hollywood
1935—Life Begins at Forty
1935—$10 Raise
1935—In Old Kentucky
1935—Show Them No Mercy
1935—Music is Magic
1936—The Crime of Doctor Forbes
1936—A Message to Garcia
1936—Can This be Dixie?
1937—Nancy Steele is Missing
1937—Love under Fire
1938—The Goldwyn Follies
1938—Battle of Broadway
1938—Hold that Co-ed
1939—You Can't Cheat an Honest Man
1939—Destry Rides Again
1940—The Ghost Breakers
1940—When the Daltons Rode
1941—Pot O' Gold
1941—Texas
1942—Valley of the Sun
1942—The Forest Rangers
1942—Star Spangled Rhythm
1943—True to Life
1943—Riding High
1944—And the Angels Sing
1945—Murder He Says
1945—Incendiary Blonde
1946—The Blue Dahlia

1946—Monsieur Beaucaire
1947—The Perils of Pauline
1947—Variety Girl
1948—Hazard
1948—Tap Roots
1949—My Friend Irma
1950—Fancy Pants
1950—Never a Dull Moment
1951—A Millionaire for Christy
1952—The Savage
1953—Off Limits
1953—Scared Stiff
1953—Houdini
1953—Money From Home
1954—Red Garters
1954—Duel in the Jungle
1954—Destry
1955—The Second Greatest Sex
1956—Pillars of the Sky
1957—The Guns of Fort Petticoat
1957—Beyond Mombasa
1957—The Sad Sack
1958—The Sheepman
1958—Imitation General
1959—The Mating Game
1959—It Started with a Kiss
1959—The Gazebo
1961—Cry for Happy
1962—The Happy Thieves
1962—How the West was Won (1 episode)
1963—Papa's Delicate Condition
1964—Dark Purpose (co-director)
1964—Advance to the Rear
1966—Boy, Did I Get a Wrong Number!
1967—Eight on the Lam
1968—The Wicked Dreams of Paula Schultz
1969—Hook, Line and Sinker

Paul Mazursky
(1929–   )

1970—Bob and Carol and Ted and Alice
1970—Alex in Wonderland
1973—Blume in Love
1974—Harry and Tonto
1976—Next Stop Greenwich Village

Mark Rydell
(1934–   )

1968—The Fox
1969—The Reivers
1972—The Cowboys
1973—Cinderella Liberty
1976—Harry and Walter Go to New York

Mervyn Le Roy
(1900–   )

1927—No Place to Go
1928—Harold Teen
1928—Flying Romeos
1929—Hot Stuff
1930—Broken Dishes
1930—Top Speed
1930—Little Caesar
1930—Little Johnny Jones
1930—Playing Around
1930—Show Girl in Hollywood
1930—Numbered Men
1931—Broad-Minded
1931—Too Young to Marry
1931—Local Boy Makes Good
1931—Tonight or Never
1932—High Pressure
1932—The Heart of New York
1932—Big City Blues
1932—Five Star Final
1932—Three on a Match
1932—I Am a Fugitive from a Chain Gang
1932—Two Seconds
1932—Tugboat Annie
1933—Gold Diggers of 1933
1933—Hi Nellie
1933—Oil for the Lamps of China
1933—Hard to Handle
1933—Elmer the Great
1933—The World Changes
1934—Heat Lightning
1934—Happiness Ahead
1934—Sweet Adeline
1934—Page Miss Glory
1935—I Found Stella Parish
1936—Anthony Adverse
1936—Three Men on a Horse

1937—They Won't Forget
1937—The King and the Chorus Girl
1938—Fools for Scandal
1940—Waterloo Bridge
1940—Escape
1941—Blossoms in the Dust
1941—Unholy Partners
1941—Johnny Eager
1942—Random Harvest
1943—Madame Curie
1944—Thirty Seconds Over Tokyo
1947—Without Reservations
1948—Homecoming
1949—Little Women
1949—Any Number Can Play
1950—East Side West Side
1951—Quo Vadis
1952—Lovely to Look At
1953—Million Dollar Mermaid
1953—Latin Lovers
1954—Rose Marie
1955—Mister Roberts (co-director)
1955—Strange Lady in Town
1956—The Bad Seed
1956—Toward the Unknown
1958—No Time for Sergeants
1959—Home Before Dark
1959—The FBI Story
1960—Wake Me When It's Over
1961—A Majority of One
1961—The Devil at Four O'Clock
1962—Gypsy
1963—Mary, Mary
1965—Moment to Moment
1969—Downstairs at Ramsey's
1970—The Thirteen Clocks

Henry Hathaway

(1898–   )

1932—Wild Horse Mesa
1933—Heritage of the Desert
1933—Under the Tonto Rim
1933—Sunset Pass
1933—Man of the Forest
1933—To the Last Man
1934—Come On Marines!
1934—The Last Round-Up
1934—The Thundering Herd
1934—The Witching Hour
1934—Now and Forever
1935—The Lives of a Bengal Lancer
1935—Peter Ibbetson
1936—The Trail of the Lonesome Pine
1936—Go West, Young Man
1937—Souls at Sea
1938—Spawn of the North
1939—The Real Glory
1940—Johnny Apollo
1940—Brigham Young
1941—The Shepherd of the Hills
1941—Sundown
1942—Ten Gentlemen from West Point
1943—China Girl
1944—Home in Indiana
1944—Wing and a Prayer
1945—Nob Hill
1945—The House on 92nd Street
1946—The Dark Corner
1946—13 Rue Madeleine
1947—Kiss of Death

1948—Call Northside 777
1949—Down to the Sea in Ships
1950—The Black Rose
1951—You're in the Navy Now
1951—Rawhide
1951—Fourteen Hours
1951—The Desert Fox
1952—Diplomatic Courier
1952—O. Henry's Full House (1 episode)
1952—Niagara
1953—White Witch Doctor
1954—Prince Valiant
1954—Garden of Evil
1954—The Racers
1955—The Bottom of the Bottle
1956—Twenty-three Paces to Baker Street
1957—Legend of the Lost
1958—From Hell to Texas
1959—Woman Obsessed
1960—Seven Thieves
1960—North to Alaska
1962—How the West Was Won
    (1 episode)
1964—Circus World
1965—The Sons of Katie Elder
1966—Nevada Smith
1967—The Last Safari
1968—5 Card Stud
1969—True Grit
1971—Raid on Rommel
1971—Shootout

Today the main difference is that pictures are made by a committee—it used to be one man—it should be one strong man, preferably the director.

Lucien Ballard, Cinematographer

Milos Forman
(1932–   )

1964—Peter and Pavla
1965—The Loves of a Blond
1967—The Fireman's Ball
1971—Taking Off
1975—One Flew Over the Cuckoo's Nest

Everybody grew up admiring Hollywood in its golden era.
Hollywood is to many directors as the Egyptian pyramids
are to architects. You have this ambition, secret ambition,
that one day you would like to go there and show them that
you can do it too. So when the opportunity opens up in
reality, of course, you have the desire but you never believe
it will happen.

Milos Forman

Franklin Schaffner
(1920–   )

1963—The Stripper
1964—The Best Man
1965—The War Lord
1968—The Double Man
1968—Planet of the Apes
1969—Patton
1971—Nicholas and Alexandra
1973—Papillon
In Production—Islands in the Stream

Norman Jewison
(1926–   )

John Schlesinger
(1926–   )

1962—A Kind of Loving
1963—Billy Liar
1965—Darling
1967—Far From the Madding Crowd
1969—Midnight Cowboy
1972—Sunday Bloody Sunday
1973—Visions of Eight (1 segment)
1975—Day of the Locust
1976—Marathon Man

Mel Brooks
(1928–   )

1968—The Producers
1970—The Twelve Chairs
1973—Blazing Saddles
1974—Young Frankenstein
1976—Silent Movie

John Frankenheimer
(1930–   )

1957—The Young Stranger
1961—The Young Savages
1962—All Fall Down
1962—The Manchurian Candidate
1962—Birdman of Alcatraz
1964—Seven Days in May
1965—The Train
1966—Seconds
1967—Grand Prix
1968—The Extraordinary Seaman
1968—The Fixer
1969—The Gypsy Moths
1970—I Walk the Line
1971—The Horsemen
1973—Impossible Object
1973—The Iceman Cometh
1974—99 and 44/100% Dead
1975—French Connection II
1976—Black Sunday

Everybody finds it so easy to be a director —how come I
find it so difficult?

Louis Malle, Director

Otto Preminger
(1906–   )

1932—Die Grosse Liebe
1936—Under Your Spell
1937—Danger, Love at Work
1943—Margin for Error
1944—In the Meantime, Darling
1944—Laura
1945—A Royal Scandal
1946—Centennial Summer
1946—Fallen Angel
1947—Forever Amber
1947—Daisy Kenyon
1948—That Lady in Ermine (co-director)
1949—The Fan
1950—Whirlpool
1950—Where the Sidewalk Ends
1951—The Thirteenth Letter
1952—Angel Face
1953—The Moon Is Blue
1954—River of No Return
1954—Carmen Jones
1955—The Court Martial of Billy Mitchell
1956—The Man with the Golden Arm
1957—Bonjour Tristesse
1957—Saint Joan
1959—Porgy and Bess
1959—Anatomy of a Murder
1960—Exodus
1961—Advise and Consent
1963—The Cardinal
1965—In Harm's Way
1965—Bunny Lake Is Missing
1967—Hurry Sundown
1968—Skidoo
1970—Tell Me That You Love Me, Junie Moon
1972—Such Good Friends
1975—Rosebud
In Production—Blood on Wheels

George Lucas
(1945–   )

1969—THX 1138
1973—American Graffiti
In Production—The Star Wars

I have personal doubts that film is an art. It may well be and
I may be wrong and people get very angry with me when I
make that suggestion. I think, it may occasionally produce
art, but I think it's made by craftsmen. It is so collaborative
in every aspect that we are all craftsmen and I kind of
shudder when I hear of a screenwriter or a director refer to
himself as an artist.

Dalton Trumbo, Screenwriter

H.C. "Hank" Potter
(1904–   )

1936—Beloved Enemy
1937—Wings Over Honolulu
1938—The Adventures of Tom Sawyer (co-director)
1938—Romance in the Dark
1938—The Shopworn Angel
1939—Blackmail
1939—The Cowboy and the Lady
1939—The Story of Vernon and Irene Castle
1940—Congo Maisie
1941—Second Chorus
1941—Hellzapoppin
1943—Victory Through Air Power (co-director)
1944—Mr. Lucky
1947—You Gotta Stay Happy
1947—The Farmer's Daughter
1948—Mr. Blandings Builds His Dream House
1948—The Time of Your Life
1948—You Gotta Stay Happy
1950—The Miniver Story
1955—Three for the Show
1957—Top Secret Affair

Steven Spielberg
(1946–   )

1973—Sugarland Express
1975—Jaws
In Production—Close Encounters of the Third Kind

I think the pictures today are so much better than they
were. I see these old pictures and they're awful, including
mine too. You were so manacled by censorship. I mean you
couldn't have a real situation, you couldn't have a happy
divorce; if you had a divorce the woman had to die or
something like that. I can't understand. I meet these
kids—they all slobber about the old films. I don't see why.

Jules Epstein, Screenwriter

Woody Allen
(1935–   )

1969—Take the Money and Run
1971—Bananas
1972—Everything You Always
       Wanted to Know About Sex
1973—Sleeper
1974—Love and Death
In Production—Woody Allen Film

Nicholas Ray
(1911–   )

1949—They Live by Night
1949—A Woman's Secret
1949—Knock On Any Door
1950—Born To Be Bad
1950—In a Lovely Place
1951—Flying Leathernecks
1951—On Dangerous Ground
1952—The Lusty Men
1954—Johnny Guitar
1955—Run for Cover
1955—Rebel without a Cause
1956—Hot Blood
1956—Bigger Than Life
1957—The True Story of Jesse James
1957—Bitter Victory
1958—Wind Across the Everglades
1958—Party Girl
1959—The Savage Innocents
1961—King of Kings
1962—55 Days at Peking
In Production—City Blues

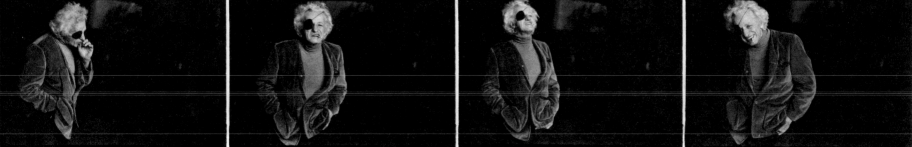

Joseph H. Lewis
(1900–   )

1937—Courage of the West
1937—Singing Outlaw
1938—Border Wolves
1938—The Spy Ring
1938—The Last Stand
1940—Two Fisted Rangers
1940—That Gang of Mine
1940—Texas Stagecoach
1940—The Man from Tumbleweeds
1940—Boys of the City
1940—Return of Wild Bill
1940—Blazing Six Shooters
1941—Pride of the Bowery
1941—The Invisible Ghost
1941—The Mad Doctor of Market Street
1942—The Boss of Hangtown Mesa
1942—Bombs over Burma
1942—Arizona Cyclone
1942—The Silver Bullet
1942—Secrets of a Co-ed
1944—Minstrel Man
1945—My Name is Julia Ross
1945—The Falcon in San Francisco
1946—So Dark the Night
1947—The Swordsman
1948—The Return of October
1949—The Undercover Man
1950—A Lady without Passport
1950—Gun Crazy
1952—Retreat, Hell!
1952—Desperate Search
1953—Cry of the Hunted
1955—The Big Combo
1955—A Lawless Street
1956—The Seventh Cavalry
1956—The Halliday Brand
1958—Terror in a Texas Town

Arthur Penn
(1922–   )

1958—The Left Handed Gun
1962—The Miracle Worker
1965—Mickey One
1966—The Chase
1967—Bonnie and Clyde
1969—Alice's Restaurant
1970—Little Big Man
1973—Visions of Eight (1 segment)
1975—Night Moves
1976—The Missouri Breaks

Allan Dwan
(1885–   )

1914—Wildflower	1936—Fifteen Maiden Lane
1916—The Good Bad Man	1937—Woman Wise
1916—The Half-Breed	1937—That I May Live
1916—Manhattan Madness	1937—One Mile from Heaven
1918—A Modern Musketeer	1937—Heidi
1918—Bound in Morocco	1938—Rebecca of Sunnybrook Farm
1919—Cheating Cheaters	1938—Josette
1919—Soldiers of Fortune	1938—Suez
1920—Luck of the Irish	1939—The Three Musketeers
1922—Robin Hood	1939—The Gorilla
1923—Glimpses of the Moon	1939—Frontier Marshall
1923—Lawful Larceny	1940—Sailor's Lady
1923—Zaza	1940—Young People
1923—Big Brother	1940—Trail of the Vigilantes
1924—A Society Scandal	1941—Rise and Shine
1924—Manhandled	1941—Look Who's Laughing
1924—Her Love Story	1942—Friendly Enemies
1924—Wages of Virtue	1942—Here We Go Again
1924—Argentine Love	1943—Around the World
1925—Night Life of New York	1944—Up in Mabel's Room
1925—The Coast of Folly	1944—Abroad With Two Yanks
1925—Stage Struck	1945—Brewster's Millions
1926—Sea Horses	1946—Getting Gertie's Garter
1926—Padlocked	1946—Rendezvous with Annie
1926—Summer Bachelors	1947—Northwest Outpost
1926—Tin Gods	1947—Calendar Girl
1927—The Joy Girl	1947—Driftwood
1927—West Point	1948—The Inside Story
1927—East Side, West Side	1949—The Sands of Iwo Jima
1927—The Music Master	1949—Angel in Exile
1927—French Dressing	1950—Surrender
1928—The Big Noise	1951—Belle le Grand
1929—The Iron Mask	1952—The Wild Blue Yonder
1929—Tide of Empire	1952—I Dream of Jeanie
1929—The Far Call	1952—Montana Belle
1929—Frozen Justice	1953—Woman They Almost Lynched
1929—South Sea Rose	1953—Sweethearts on Parade
1930—What a Widow	1954—Flight Nurse
1931—Man to Man	1954—Silver Lode
1931—Chances	1954—Passion
1931—Wicked	1955—Cattle Queen of Montana
1932—While Paris Sleeps	1955—Escape to Burma
1933—Her First Affaire	1955—Pearl of the Pacific
1933—Counsel's Opinion	1955—Tennessee's Partner
1934—The Morning After	1956—Slightly Scarlet
1934—Hollywood Party	1956—Hold Back the Night
1935—Black Sheep	1957—The River's Edge
1936—Song and Dance Man	1957—The Restless Breed
1936—Human Cargo	1958—Enchanted Island
1936—High Tension	1961—Most Dangerous Man Alive

William Keighley
(1889–   )

1932—The Match King (co-director)
1933—Ladies They Talk About (co-director)
1934—Easy to Love
1934—Journal of a Crime
1934—Dr. Monica
1934—Kansas City Princess
1934—Big Hearted Herbert
1934—Babbitt
1935—The Right to Live
1935—G Men
1935—Special Agent
1935—Stars Over Broadway
1936—The Singing Kid
1936—Bullets or Ballots
1936—The Green Pastures (co-director)
1937—God's Country and the Woman
1937—The Prince and the Pauper
1937—Varsity Show
1938—Adventures of Robin Hood (co-director)
1938—Valley of the Giants
1938—The Secrets of an Actress
1938—Brother Rat
1939—Yes, My Darling Daughter
1939—Each Dawn I Die
1940—The Fighting 69th
1940—Torrid Zone
1940—No Time For Comedy
1941—Four Mothers
1941—The Bride Came C.O.D.
1942—The Man Who Came to Dinner
1942—George Washington Slept Here
1947—Honeymoon
1948—The Street with No Name
1950—Rocky Mountain
1951—Close to My Heart
1953—The Master of Ballantrae

The artist has never been the lord of creation, he's more often been sitting outside the kitchen door you know, with his hand open waiting for a little of the good.

Dalton Trumbo, Screenwriter

Vincente Minnelli
(1913–   )

1943—Cabin in the Sky
1943—I Dood It
1944—Meet Me in St. Louis
1944—The Clock
1945—Yolanda and the Thief
1945—Ziegfeld Follies
1946—Undercurrent
1947—The Pirate
1949—Madame Bovary
1950—Father of the Bride
1951—Father's Little Dividend
1951—An American in Paris
1952—The Bad and the Beautiful
1952—The Story of Three Loves (1 episode)
1953—The Band Wagon
1954—The Long, Long Trailer
1954—Brigadoon
1955—Kismet
1955—The Cobweb
1956—Lust for Life
1956—Tea and Sympathy
1957—Designing Woman
1958—Gigi
1958—The Reluctant Debutante
1958—Some Came Running
1959—Home from the Hill
1960—Bells Are Ringing
1962—The Four Horsemen of the Apocalypse
1962—Two Weeks in Another Town
1963—The Courtship of Eddie's Father
1965—Goodbye Charlie
1965—The Sandpiper
1970—On A Clear Day You Can See Forever
1976—A Matter of Time

Stanley Kramer
(1913–   )

1955—Not as a Stranger
1957—The Pride and the Passion
1958—The Defiant Ones
1959—On the Beach
1960—Inherit the Wind
1961—Judgment at Nuremberg
1963—It's a Mad, Mad, Mad, Mad World
1965—Ship of Fools
1967—Guess Who's Coming to Dinner?
1969—The Secret of Santa Vittoria
1971—R.P.M.
1971—Bless the Beasts and Children
1973—Oklahoma Crude
In Production—The Domino Principle

Robert Wise
(1914–   )

1944—Mademoiselle Fifi
1944—Curse of the Cat People
1945—The Body Snatcher
1946—A Game of Death
1946—Criminal Court
1947—Born to Kill
1947—Mystery in Mexico
1948—Blood on the Moon
1949—The Set-Up
1950—Three Secrets
1950—Two Flags West
1951—The House on Telegraph Hill
1951—The Day the Earth Stood Still
1952—The Captive City
1952—Destination Gobi
1952—Something for the Birds
1952—Desert Rats
1953—So Big
1954—Executive Suite
1955—Helen of Troy
1956—Tribute to a Bad Man
1956—Somebody Up There Likes Me
1957—Until They Sail
1957—This Could Be the Night
1958—Run Silent Run Deep
1958—I Want to Live!
1959—Odds Against Tomorrow
1961—West Side Story
1962—Two for the Seesaw
1963—The Haunting
1965—The Sound of Music
1966—The Sand Pebbles
1968—Star!
1971—The Andromeda Strain
1973—Two People
1976—The Hindenburg
In Production—Audrey Rose

Andy Warhol
(1928–   )

1963—Sleep
1965—Vinyl
1965—My Hustler
1965—The Life of Juanita Castro
1966—Chelsea Girls
1967—Bikeboy
1969—Blue Movie

Melvin Frank
(1917–   )

1950—The Reformer and the Redhead (co-director)
1951—Strictly Dishonorable (co-director)
1951—Callaway Went Thataway (co-director)
1952—Above and Beyond (co-director)
1954—Knock on Wood (co-director)
1956—The Court Jester (co-director)
1956—That Certain Feeling (co-director)
1959—The Jayhawkers
1960—Li'l Abner
1960—The Facts of Life
1968—Buona Sera Mrs. Campbell
1972—A Touch of Class
1974—Prisoner of Second Avenue
1976—The Duchess and the Dirtwater Fox

Francis Ford Coppola
(1939–   )

1963—Dementia
1967—You're a Big Boy Now
1968—Finian's Rainbow
1969—The Rain People
1972—The Godfather
1973—The Conversation
1974—Godfather II
In Production—Apocalypse Now

Fritz Lang
(1890–1976)

1919—Halbblut
1919—Der Herr der Liebe
1919—Die Spinnen-I
1919—Hara Kiri
1920—Die Spinnen-II
1920—Das Wandernde Bild
1921—Vier um die Frau
1921—Der Mude Tod
1922—Dr. Mabuse der Spieler (I & II)
1924—Die Niebelungen (I & II)
1926—Metropolis
1927—Spione
1928—Die Frau im Mond
1931—M
1932—Das Testament von Dr. Mabuse
1933—Liliom
1936—Fury
1937—You Only Live Once
1938—You and Me
1940—The Return of Frank James
1941—Western Union

1941—Man Hunt
1943—Hangmen Also Die
1944—The Woman in the Window
1944—Ministry of Fear
1945—Scarlet Street
1946—Cloak and Dagger
1948—The Secret Beyond the Door
1949—House by the River
1951—An American Guerrilla
     in the Philippines
1952—Rancho Notorious
1952—Clash by Night
1952—The Blue Gardenia
1953—The Big Heat
1954—Human Desire
1955—Moonfleet
1955—While the City Sleeps
1956—Beyond a Reasonable Doubt
1959—Das Indische Grabmal
1959—Der Tiger von Eschnapur
1960—Die Tausend Augen des Dr. Mabuse

Gilbert Cates
(1924–   )

1966—Rings Around the World
1969—I Never Sang for My Father
1973—The Affair
1973—Summer Wishes, Winter Dreams
1976—Dragonfly
In Production—Limehouse

I dislike people who ask "What is your movie about?" when
A. it hasn't been seen, or B. I haven't finished it yet. What's
it about? There are only thirty-six plots in the whole world
so it's got to be one of those.

Nicolas Roeg, Director

Hal Ashby
(1936–   )

Sidney J. Furie
(1933–   )

1957—A Dangerous Age
1958—A Cool Sound from Hell
1960—The Snake Woman
1961—Doctor Blood's Coffin
1961—During One Night
1961—Three on a Spree
1961—The Young Ones
1962—The Boys
1963—The Leather Boys
1964—Wonderful Life
1965—The Ipcress File
1965—Day of the Arrow
1966—The Appaloosa
1967—The Naked Runner
1969—The Lawyer
1970—Little Fauss and Big Halsy
1972—Lady Sings the Blues
1973—Hit
1974—Sheila Levine Is Dead
          and Living in New York
1976—Gable and Lombard

William Friedkin
(1939–   )

George Cukor
(1899–   )

1930—The Royal Family of Broadway (co-director)
1930—Virtuous Sin (co-director)
1930—Grumpy (co-director)
1930—Tarnished Lady
1931—Girls About Town
1932—One Hour with You (co-director)
1932—What Price Hollywood
1932—A Bill of Divorcement
1932—Rockabye
1933—Our Betters
1933—Dinner at Eight
1933—Little Women
1934—David Copperfield
1935—Sylvia Scarlett
1936—Romeo and Juliet
1936—Camille
1938—Holiday
1939—Zaza
1939—The Women
1940—Susan and God
1940—The Philadelphia Story
1941—A Woman's Face
1941—Two-Faced Woman
1942—Her Cardboard Lover

1943—Keeper of the Flame
1944—Gaslight
1944—Winged Victory
1947—A Double Life
1949—Adam's Rib
1949—Edward, My Son
1950—A Life of Her Own
1950—Born Yesterday
1952—The Model and the Marriage Broker
1952—The Marrying Kind
1952—Pat and Mike
1953—The Actress
1953—It Should Happen to You
1954—A Star is Born
1956—Bhowani Junction
1957—Les Girls
1957—Wild is the Wind
1959—Heller in Pink Tights
1961—Let's Make Love
1962—The Chapman Report
1964—My Fair Lady
1969—Justine
1973—Travels with My Aunt
1976—Bluebird
In Production—Vicky

Samuel Fuller
(1911–   )

1949—I Shot Jesse James
1950—The Baron of Arizona
1951—Fixed Bayonets
1951—The Steel Helmet
1952—Park Row
1952—Pickup on South Street
1954—Hell and High Water
1955—House of Bamboo
1955—Run of the Arrow
1956—China Gate
1957—Forty Guns
1959—Verboten
1959—The Crimson Kimono
1960—Underworld USA
1962—Merrill's Marauders
1964—Shock Corridor
1966—The Naked Kiss
1967—Shark
1973—Riata
1973—Dead Pigeon on Beethoven Street

Twenty five years from now, todays heros, heroines, villains
and car chases will be the next Keystones; and tomorrows
children will make films of the "Splendid 70s".

Sam Fuller

Delmer Daves
(1904–   )

1943—Destination Tokyo
1944—The Very Thought of You
1944—Hollywood Canteen
1945—Pride of the Marines
1947—The Red House
1947—Dark Passage
1948—To the Victor
1949—A Kiss in the Dark
1949—Task Force
1950—Broken Arrow
1951—Bird of Paradise
1952—Return of the Texan
1953—Treasure of the Golden Condor
1953—Never Let Me Go
1954—Demetrius and the Gladiators
1954—Drum Beat
1956—Jubal
1956—The Last Wagon
1957—3:10 to Yuma
1958—Cowboy
1958—Kings Go Forth
1958—The Badlanders
1959—The Hanging Tree
1960—A Summer Place
1961—Susan Slade
1961—Parrish
1962—Spencer's Mountain
1962—Rome Adventure
1964—Youngblood Hawke
1965—The Battle of the Villa Fiorita

Russ Meyer
(1922–   )

1959—The Immoral Mr. Teas
1961—Eve and the Handyman
1962—Eroticon
1962—Mondo Freudo
1962—Wild Gals of the Naked West
1963—Europe in the Flesh
1964—Lorna
1965—Mud Honey
1965—Motor Psycho
1966—Mondo Topless
1966—Faster Pussy Cat, Kill, Kill!
1967—Good Morning... and Goodbye
1967—Common Law Cabin
1968—Vixen
1968—Finders Keepers, Lovers Weepers
1969—Cherry, Harry and Raquel
1970—Beyond the Valley of the Dolls
1971—The Seven Minutes
1972—Blacksnake
1975—Russ Meyer's Super Vixens

Richard Brooks
(1912–   )

1950—Crisis
1951—The Light Touch
1952—Deadline U.S.A.
1952—Battle Circus
1954—The Last Time I Saw Paris
1954—Take the High Ground
1954—The Flame and the Flesh
1955—The Blackboard Jungle
1956—The Last Hunt
1956—The Catered Affair
1957—Something of Value
1958—The Brothers Karamazov
1958—Cat on a Hot Tin Roof
1960—Elmer Gantry
1962—Sweet Bird of Youth
1965—Lord Jim
1966—The Professionals
1967—In Cold Blood
1970—Happy Ending
1972—Dollars
1975—Bite the Bullet

Peter Bogdanovich
(1939–   )

1968—Targets
1971—The Last Picture Show
1972—What's Up Doc?
1973—Paper Moon
1974—Daisy Miller
1975—At Long Last Love
1976—Nickelodeon

Melvin Van Peebles
(1932–   )

1967—The Story of a Three-day Pass
1969—Watermelon Man
1970—Sweet Sweetback's Baad Asssss Song

I make a film like I cook for friends. I hope they like it, but
if they don't, I'm prepared to enjoy it all by myself.

Melvin Van Peebles

Roger Corman
(1926–   )

1955—Five Guns West
1955—Apache Woman
1956—Swamp Woman
1956—Gunslinger
1956—The Day the World Ended
1956—It Conquered the World
1957—Not of this Earth
1957—Attack of the Crab Monsters
1957—Rock All Night
1957—The Undead
1958—Sorority Girl
1958—Machine Gun Kelly
1958—I, Mobster
1958—Teenage Caveman
1959—A Bucket of Blood
1959—The Cry Baby Killer
1959—Wasp Woman
1960—The House of Usher
1960—The Little Shop of Horrors
1960—Last Woman on Earth
1961—The Creature from the Haunted Sea
1961—The Pit and the Pendulum
1961—The Intruder
1962—The Premature Burial
1962—Tales of Terror
1962—Tower of London
1963—The Raven
1963—The Young Racers
1963—X—The Man with the X-Ray Eyes
1963—The Haunted Palace
1964—The Secret Invasion
1964—The Masque of the Red Death
1965—The Tomb of Ligeia
1966—The Wild Angels
1967—The St. Valentine's Day Massacre
1967—The Trip
1970—Bloody Mama
1971—Von Richthofen and Brown
1971—Gas-s-s

Billy Wilder
(1906–   )

1933—Mauvaise Graine (co-director)
1942—The Major and the Minor
1943—Five Graves to Cairo
1944—Double Indemnity
1945—The Lost Weekend
1947—The Emperor Waltz
1949—A Foreign Affair
1951—Sunset Boulevard
1951—Ace in the Hole
1953—Stalag 17
1954—Sabrina
1955—The Seven Year Itch
1957—The Spirit of St. Louis
1957—Love in the Afternoon
1958—Witness for the Prosecution
1959—Some Like It Hot
1960—The Apartment
1961—One, Two, Three
1963—Irma La Douce
1964—Kiss Me, Stupid
1966—The Fortune Cookie
1970—The Private Life of Sherlock Holmes
1972—Avanti
1974—The Front Page

Fred Zinnemann
(1907–   )

1935—The Wave
1942—Kid Glove Killer
1942—Eyes in the Night
1944—The Seventh Cross
1946—Little Mister Jim
1947—My Brother Talks to Horses
1948—The Search
1949—Act of Violence
1950—The Men
1951—Teresa
1952—High Noon
1953—The Member of the Wedding
1953—From Here to Eternity
1955—Oklahoma!
1957—A Hatful of Rain
1958—The Nun's Story
1960—The Sundowners
1963—Behold a Pale Horse
1966—A Man for All Seasons
1973—The Day of the Jackal
In Production—Julia

My only quarrel with the new Hollywood is with infantilism
masquerading as sophistication. It is my somewhat optimistic
hope that a new generation of filmmakers will outgrow this
preoccupation with animated graffiti, and learn the ABC's of
entertainment—which is at least the basis of that rare
commodity, art. Indeed, I feel there is a good chance that
these young will learn, from life as well as from art.

Raoul Walsh, Director

Mike Nichols
(1931–   )

1966—Who's Afraid of Virginia Woolf?
1967—The Graduate
1970—Catch 22
1971—Carnal Knowledge
1973—The Day of the Dolphin

William Wellman
(1896–1975)

1923—The Man Who Won	1934—Looking for Trouble
1923—Second Hand Love	1934—Stingaree
1923—Big Dan	1934—The President Vanishes
1923—Cupid's Fireman	1935—Small Town Girl
1924—The Vagabond Trail	1935—Call of the Wild
1924—Not a Drum Was Heard	1936—Robin Hood of Eldorado
1924—The Circus Cowboy	1937—Nothing Sacred
1924—When Husbands Flirt	1937—A Star is Born
1924—The Boob	1938—Men With Wings
1924—The Cat's Pajamas	1939—Beau Geste
1926—You Never Know Women	1939—The Light That Failed
1927—Wings	1940—Reaching for the Sun
1928—The Legion of the Condemned	1942—The Great Man's Lady
1928—Ladies of the Mob	1942—The Ox Bow Incident
1928—Beggars of Life	1942—Roxie Hart
1929—Chinatown Nights	1942—Thunder Birds
1929—The Man I Love	1943—Buffalo Bill
1929—Woman Trap	1943—Lady of Burlesque
1930—Dangerous Paradise	1945—This Man's Navy
1930—Young Eagles	1945—Story of GI Joe
1930—Maybe It's Love	1946—Gallant Journey
1931—Other Men's Women	1946—Magic Town
1931—The Public Enemy	1948—Happy Years
1931—Night Nurse	1948—The Iron Curtain
1931—The Star Witness	1948—Yellow Sky
1931—Safe in Hell	1949—Battleground
1932—The Hatchet Man	1950—The Next Voice You Hear
1932—So Big	1950—Westward the Women
1932—Love is a Racket	1951—It's a Big Country (1 episode)
1932—The Purchase Price	1951—Across the Wide Missouri
1932—The Conquerers	1952—My Man and I
1933—Frisco Jenny	1953—Island in the Sky
1933—Central Airport	1954—The High and the Mighty
1933—Lilly Turner	1954—Track of the Cat
1933—Midnight Mary	1955—Blood Alley
1933—Heroes for Sale	1956—Goodbye My Lady
1933—Wild Boys of the Road	1958—Darby's Rangers
1933—College Coach	1958—Lafayette Escadrille

George Roy Hill
(1922–   )

1963—Period of Adjustment
1963—Toys in the Attic
1964—The World of Henry Orient
1966—Hawaii
1967—Thoroughly Modern Millie
1969—Butch Cassidy and the Sundance Kid
1972—Slaughterhouse Five
1973—The Thug
1973—The Sting
1974—The Great Waldo Pepper
In Production—Slap Shot

Tay Garnett
(1895–   )

1928—Celebrity
1928—The Spieler
1929—Flying Fools
1929—Oh Yeah!
1930—Officer O'Brien
1930—Her Man
1931—Bad Company
1932—One Way Passage
1932—Prestige
1932—Okay America
1933—Destination Unknown
1933—SOS Iceberg
1935—China Seas
1935—She Couldn't Take It
1935—Professional Soldier
1937—Love Is News
1937—Slave Ship
1937—Stand-In
1938—Joy of Living
1938—Trade Winds
1939—Eternally Yours
1940—Slightly Honorable

1940—Seven Sinners
1941—Cheers for Miss Bishop
1942—My Favorite Spy
1943—Bataan
1943—The Cross of Lorraine
1944—Mrs. Parkington
1945—The Valley of Decision
1946—The Postman Always Rings Twice
1947—Wild Harvest
1949—A Connecticut Yankee in King
        Arthur's Court
1950—The Fireball
1951—Soldiers Three
1951—Cause for Alarm
1952—One Minute to Zero
1953—Main Street to Broadway
1955—The Black Knight
1958—Seven Wonders of the World
1960—The Night Fighters
1963—Cattle King
1973—The Temper Tramp
1975—Challenge to Be Free

Bob Rafelson
(1935–   )

1968—Head
1971—Five Easy Pieces
1972—The King of Marvin Gardens
1976—Stay Hungry

Abe Polonsky
(1910–   )

1948—Force of Evil
1969—Tell Them Willie Boy Is Here
1971—Romance of a Horse Thief

Budd Boetticher
(1916–   )

Arthur Hiller
(1924–   )

1957—The Careless Years
1963—The Flight of the White Stallions
1964—The Americanization of Emily
1966—Promise Her Anything
1966—Tobruk
1966—Penelope
1967—The Tiger Makes Out
1969—Popi
1969—The Out-of-Towners
1970—Love Story
1970—Plaza Suite
1971—The Hospital
1972—Man of la Mancha
1974—The Crazy World of Julius Vrooder
1974—The Man in the Glass Booth
1976—W.C. Fields and Me
In Production—The Silver Streak

King Vidor
(1894–   )

1918—The Turn in the Road
1919—Better Times
1919—The Other Half
1919—Poor Relations
1919—The Jack Knife Man
1920—The Family Honor
1921—The Sky Pilot
1921—Love Never Dies
1921—Conquering the Women
1921—Woman, Wake Up
1922—The Real Adventure
1922—Dusk to Dawn
1922—Alice Adams
1922—Peg o' My Heart
1923—The Woman of Bronze
1923—Three Wise Fools
1923—Wild Oranges
1923—Happiness
1924—Wine of Youth
1924—His Hour
1924—Wife of the Centaur
1925—Proud Flesh
1925—The Big Parade
1925—La Bohème
1926—Bardelys the Magnificent
1928—The Patsy
1928—The Crowd
1928—Show People

1929—Hallelujah!
1930—Not So Dumb
1930—Billy the Kid
1931—Street Scene
1931—The Champ
1932—Bird of Paradise
1932—Cynara
1933—The Stranger's Return
1934—Our Daily Bread
1934—The Wedding Night
1935—So Red the Rose
1936—The Texas Rangers
1937—Stella Dallas
1938—The Citadel
1939—Northwest Passage
1940—Comrade X
1941—H.M. Pulham, Esq.
1944—An American Romance
1946—Duel in the Sun
1948—On Our Merry Way (co-director)
1949—The Fountainhead
1949—Beyond the Forest
1951—Lightning Strikes Twice
1952—Japanese War Bride
1952—Ruby Gentry
1955—The Man Without a Star
1956—War and Peace
1959—Solomon and Sheba

John Cassavetes
(1929–   )

1961—Shadows
1962—Too Late Blues
1962—A Child is Waiting
1968—Faces
1970—Husbands
1971—Minnie and Moskowitz
1974—A Woman under the Influence
1976—The Killing of a Chinese Bookie

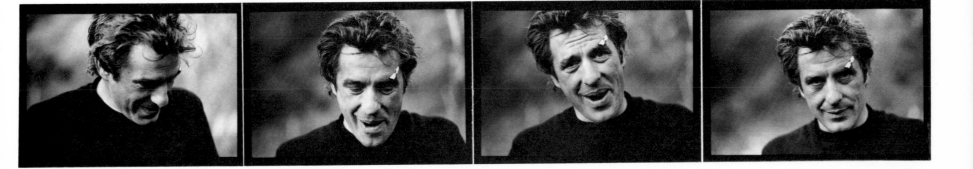

Edward Dmytryk
(1908–   )

1935—The Hawk
1939—Television Spy
1940—Emergency Squad
1940—Golden Gloves
1940—Mystery Sea Raider
1940—Her First Romance
1941—The Devil Commands
1941—Under Age
1941—Sweetheart of the Campus
1941—Blonde from Singapore
1941—Confessions of
        Boston Blackie
1941—Secrets of the Lone Wolf
1942—Counter Espionage
1942—Seven Miles From Alcatraz
1943—Hitler's Children
1943—The Falcon Strikes Back
1943—Behind the Rising Sun
1943—Captive Wild Woman
1944—Tender Comrade
1944—Murder My Sweet
1945—Back to Bataan
1946—Cornered
1946—Till the End of Time
1947—Crossfire
1947—So Well Remembered

1948—The Hidden Room
1949—Give Us This Day
1952—Mutiny
1952—The Sniper
1952—Eight Iron Men
1953—The Juggler
1954—The Caine Mutiny
1954—Broken Lance
1954—The End of the Affair
1955—Soldier of Fortune
1955—The Left Hand of God
1956—The Mountain
1957—Raintree County
1958—The Young Lions
1959—Warlock
1959—The Blue Angel
1961—The Reluctant Saint
1962—A Walk on the Wild Side
1963—The Carpetbaggers
1964—Where Love Has Gone
1965—Mirage
1966—Alvarez Kelly
1968—Anzio
1968—Shalako
1972—Bluebeard
1975—The Human Factor

Joseph L. Mankiewicz
(1909–   )

"Lubitsch once said to me, concerning the director's general
approach to his film, that by and large he should make it for
himself, as a film *he* would buy a ticket to see—and then
pray for millions of people to agree with him."

Joseph L. Mankiewicz

Robert Aldrich
(1918–   )

1953—The Big Leaguer
1954—The World for Ransom
1954—Apache
1954—Vera Cruz
1955—Kiss Me Deadly
1955—The Big Knife
1956—Autumn Leaves
1957—Attack!
1959—Ten Seconds to Hell
1959—The Angry Hills
1960—The Last Sunset
1962—Whatever Happened to Baby Jane?
1963—Sodom and Gomorrah (co-director)
1963—Four for Texas
1965—Hush...Hush, Sweet Charlotte
1965—The Flight of the Phoenix
1966—The Dirty Dozen
1968—The Killing of Sister George
1968—The Legend of Lylah Clare
1969—Too Late the Hero
1971—The Grissom Gang
1972—Ulzana's Raid
1973—Emperor of the North Pole
1974—The Longest Yard
1975—Hustle
1976—The Choirboys
In Production—Twilight's Last Gleaming

Sam Peckinpah
(1926–   )

George Stevens
(1904–1975)

1933—Cohens and Kellys In Trouble
1934—Bachelor Bait
1934—Kentucky Kernels
1934—Laddie
1934—The Nitwits
1934—Alice Adams
1935—Annie Oakley
1936—Swing Time
1937—A Damsel in Distress
1937—Quality Street
1938—Vivacious Lady
1939—Gunga Din
1940—Vigil in the Night
1940—Penny Serenade
1941—Woman of the Year
1942—Talk of the Town
1943—The More the Merrier
1947—I Remember Mama
1951—A Place in the Sun
1952—Something to Live For
1953—Shane
1956—Giant
1959—The Diary of Anne Frank
1965—The Greatest Story Ever Told
1969—The Only Game in Town

Frank Capra
(1897–   )

1926—The Strong Man
1927—Long Pants
1927—For the Love of Mike
1928—That Certain Feeling
1928—So This is Love
1928—The Matinee Idol
1928—The Way of the Strong
1928—Say It with Sables
1928—Submarine
1928—Power of the Press
1929—The Younger Generation
1929—The Donovan Affair
1929—Flight
1930—Ladies of Leisure
1930—Rain or Shine
1931—Dirigible
1931—Miracle Woman
1931—Forbidden
1932—Platinum Blonde
1932—American Madness
1932—The Bitter Tea of General Yen
1933—Lady for a Day
1934—It Happened One Night
1934—Broadway Bill
1936—Mr. Deeds Goes to Town
1937—Lost Horizon
1938—You Can't Take It with You
1939—Mr. Smith Goes to Washington
1941—Meet John Doe
1944—Arsenic and Old Lace
1946—It's a Wonderful Life
1948—State of the Union
1950—Riding High
1951—Here Comes the Groom
1959—A Hole in the Head
1961—A Pocketful of Miracles

Lewis Milestone
(1895–   )

1925—Seven Sinners
1926—The Cave Man
1926—The New Klondike
1927—Two Arabian Knights
1928—The Garden of Eden
1928—The Racket
1929—Betrayal
1929—New York Nights
1930—All Quiet on the Western Front
1931—The Front Page
1932—Rain
1933—Hallelujah, I'm A Bum
1934—The Captain Hates the Sea
1935—Paris in Spring
1936—Anything Goes
1936—The General Died at Dawn
1939—Of Mice and Men
1940—Night of Nights
1940—Lucky Partners
1941—My Life With Caroline
1941—Edge of Darkness
1943—North Star
1944—The Purple Heart
1946—The Strange Love of Martha Ivers
1946—A Walk in the Sun
1947—No Minor Vices
1948—Arch of Triumph
1948—The Red Pony
1951—Halls of Montezuma
1952—Kangaroo
1952—Les Miserables
1953—Melba
1954—They Who Dare
1955—The Widow
1959—Pork Chop Hill
1961—Ocean's Eleven
1962—Mutiny on the Bounty

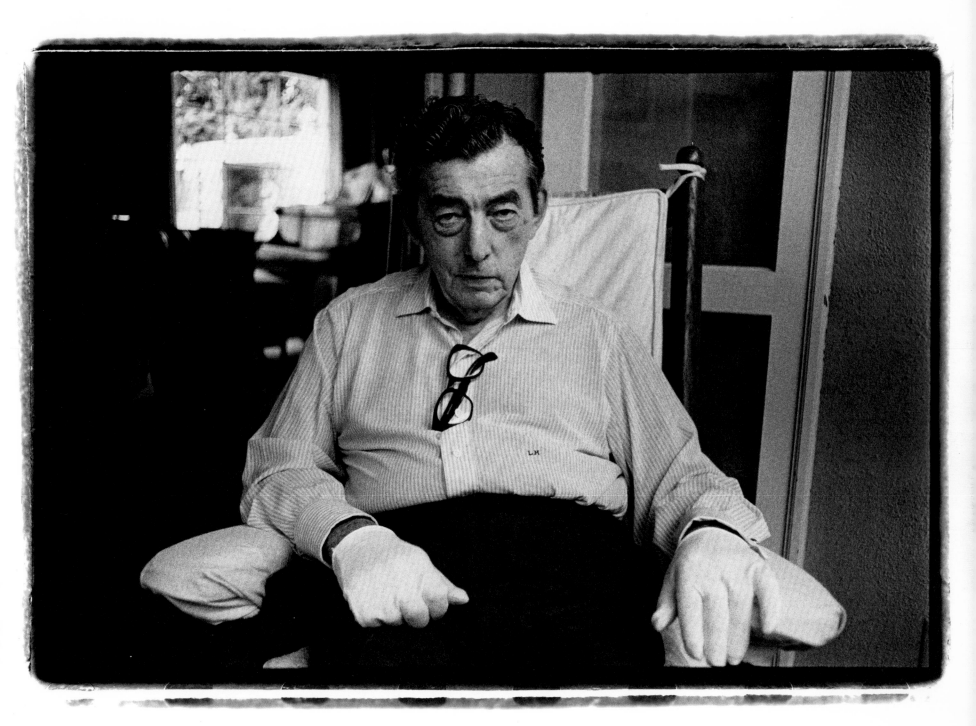

Alfred Hitchcock
(1899–   )

1925—The Pleasure Garden
1925—The Mountain Eagle
1926—The Lodger
1927—Downhill
1927—Easy Virtue
1927—The Ring
1928—The Farmer's Wife
1928—Champagne
1929—The Manxman
1929—Blackmail
1929—Harmony Heaven
1930—Elstree Calling (2 episodes)
1930—Juno and the Paycock
1930—Murder
1931—The Skin Game
1931—East of Shanghai
1932—Number Seventeen
1933—Waltzes from Vienna
1934—The Man Who Knew
    Too Much
1935—The Thirty Nine Steps
1936—Secret Agent
1937—Sabotage
1937—Young and Innocent
1938—The Lady Vanishes
1939—Jamaica Inn
1940—Rebecca
1940—Foreign Correspondent

1941—Mr. and Mrs. Smith
1941—Suspicion
1942—Saboteur
1943—Shadow of a Doubt
1943—Lifeboat
1945—Spellbound
1946—Notorious
1947—The Paradine Case
1948—Rope
1949—Under Capricorn
1950—Stage Fright
1951—Strangers on a Train
1953—I Confess
1954—Dial M for Murder
1954—Rear Window
1955—To Catch a Thief
1955—The Trouble with Harry
1956—The Man Who Knew Too Much
1957—The Wrong Man
1958—Vertigo
1959—North by Northwest
1960—Psycho
1963—The Birds
1964—Marnie
1966—Torn Curtain
1969—Topaz
1972—Frenzy
1976—Family Plot

"A touch of clairvoyance would have come in handy... But you're never clairvoyant... you have no way of knowing, actually, that the film won't wind up on its ass. So you go right on, functioning as you always have. You've done your best on the hits; you've done your best on the flops, too. In the end, the outcome seems to depend upon a magical intangible that no one has ever been able to define—much less control. I wouldn't have it any other way. That intangible is what the theater is all about."

Joseph L. Mankiewicz, Director